IR

SO-AWX-742

Katie Woo's

Funny Friends and Family Jokes

Based on characters created by Fran Manushkin

edited by Blake Hoena

illustrated by Tammie Lyon

PICTURE WINDOW BOOKS
a capstone imprint

Katie Woo is published by Picture Window Books,
A Capstone Imprint
1710 Roe Crest Drive
North Mankato, Minnesota 56003
www.mycapstone.com

Library of Congress Cataloging-in-Publication Data is available on the Library of Congress website.

ISBN: 978-1-5158-0973-9 (library binding)
ISBN: 978-1-5158-0977-7 (paperback)
ISBN: 978-1-5158-0989-0 (eBook PDF)

Summary: Katie Woo has some of the funniest friends and family around, so it is no surprise that she has a joke book filled with laughs all about them. Her jokes about JoJo, her mom and dad, and her grandparents are sure to make you giggle. Then learn how to tell jokes yourself with Katie's tips.

Designer: Kayla Dohmen

Printed in the United States of America.
010045S17

Table of Contents

Dizzy **DAD** Jokes

What do you get when your dad falls through the ice?

A POP-sicle.

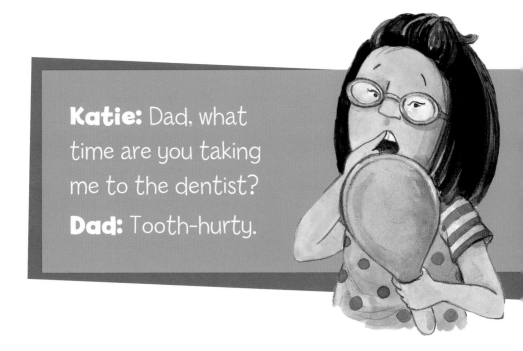

Katie: Dad, what time are you taking me to the dentist?

Dad: Tooth-hurty.

Katie: Dad, did you know that there's a shoe in the sink?

Dad: Yeah, it's clogged.

JoJo: What are you doing after school today?

Katie: Going home to practice on my drum set.

JoJo: I didn't know you played the drums.

Katie: I don't, but every time I bang on them my dad pays me $5 to stop!

Katie: Are we having soup for dinner tonight?

Dad: I SOUP-pose.

Katie: Dad, how does the turkey smell?

Dad: With its beak.

How do you make a tissue dance?

Put a little boogie in it.

What did the baby corn say when it was afraid?

"I want my POP-corn."

Katie: Dad, can you put my shoes on?

Dad: Sure, but I don't think they'll fit me.

Katie: Dad, I'm hungry.

Dad: Hi, Hungry. Nice to meet you.

Katie: Dad, I'm serious.

Dad: But I thought you were Hungry!

I stayed up all night wondering where the sun went. Then it dawned on me.

Amusing **MOM** Jokes

What did the momma tomato say to the baby tomato?

"Come on, ketch-up."

What did the momma broom say when she woke up late?

"I over-SWEPT."

Knock, knock.

Who's there?

Stranger.

Stranger who?

Didn't your mother tell you not to talk to strangers?

Mom: Katie, has your tooth stopped hurting?

Katie: I don't know. The dentist kept it.

When I asked my mom to raise my allowance, she said, "Do you think I'm made of money?" I replied, "Isn't that what M.O.M. stands for?"

Goofy **GRANDPARENT** Jokes

Why was Grandpa sitting on his watch?

He wanted to be on time.

Katie: Grandpa, were you afraid of the dark when you were my age?

Grandpa: Yes, I was. And way back when I was your age, I was also afraid of dinosaurs.

Knock, knock.
Who's there?
Honeycomb.
Honeycomb who?
Honeycomb your hair.

About 15 minutes after I sit down to watch the news.

Grandma, when is your bedtime?

What did Grandpa say when a dog sat on his hat?

"DOG-ON it." (Doggone it)

Katie: How old is Grandpa?

Grandma: I don't know, but I've sure had him a long time.

FOOD, FUN, AND FRIENDS

Why did the cookie
go to the doctor?

It was feeling crumby.

What do you get when you
cross a cow with a duck?

Milk and quackers.

What do you call
a fake noodle?

An im-pasta.

How do you make a milkshake?

Scare it!

Knock, knock.
Who's there?
Cash.
Cash who?
Oh, you're such a nut!

What did one eye say to the other eye?

"Something between us smells."

What do you call a moody piece of fruit?

A crab apple.

Which state has the smallest soft drink?

Mini-soda.

JoJo: Katie, want to hear a joke about pizza?

Katie: No, it's probably cheesy.

Knock, knock.
Who's there?
Tennis.
Tennis who?
TEN-nis my favorite number!

Why are best friends like monkeys?

They like you, especially when
you act bananas!

What kind of fruit is never lonely?

Pears.

Why did the cantaloupe jump into the lake?

It wanted to be a watermelon.

Once you lick the frosting off a cupcake, it's just a muffin.

Funnies for **FAMILY** Gatherings

What do you call a peanut in a space suit?

An astro-NUT!

Why is it bad to step on a banana?

You might hurt its PEEL-ings.

Why did the clown go to the doctor?

He was feeling funny.

Knock, knock.
Who's there?
Figs.
Figs who?
**Figs the doorbell.
It's broken!**

How are families like pieces of fudge?

Most are filled with nuts.

Did you hear about the angry pancake?

It just flipped!

Knock, knock.
Who's there?
Noble.
Noble who?
There's noble (no bell), so I had to knock!

How do you fix a broken tomato?

With tomato paste.

Katie: Did you hear about the kidnapping at the park today?

JoJo: No, what happened?

Katie: His mom had to wake him up.

Knock, knock.
Who's there?
Lettuce.
Lettuce who?
Lettuce in, please.

Why did the dinosaur cross the road?

Because there were no chickens yet.

HOW
TO TELL A
JOKE

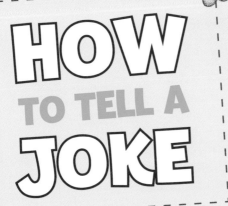

Even the funniest jokes can get groans if you don't tell them right. Here are my best joke-telling tips!

Know your audience—
Everybody has a different sense of humor. That means different things make different people laugh. My friends like jokes about school and gross things. My grandparents think jokes about old stuff are a hoot. So I pick jokes that my audience is sure to laugh at.

by Katie Woo

Know your material—I memorize my jokes. I like to stand in front of a mirror and practice the joke until I know it by heart. That way I know I'll do a good job when I'm ready to tell it to someone.

Timing—Most jokes have two parts. The setup says what the joke is about, and the punch line is the funny part. Here's an example:

Setup: What do you call a moody piece of fruit?
Punch line: A crab apple.

After I say the setup, I'm always excited to blurt out the punch line right away. But I stop myself. Instead, I take a deep breath and slowly count "one-banana, two-banana" in my head. That way my audience has time to think about the joke. If they don't answer by two-banana, then I shout the punch line. Ha!

DISCARD